Dian
FOSSEY

Liz Gogerly

Wayland
an imprint of Hodder Children's Books

© 2002 White-Thomson Publishing Ltd

Produced for Hodder Wayland by
White-Thomson Publishing Ltd
2/3 St Andrew's Place
Lewes
BN7 1UP

Editor: Anna Lee
Designer: Malcolm Walker
Cover design: Tony Fleetwood
Picture Researcher: Shelley Noronha, Glass Onion Pictures
Map Illustrator: Tim Mayer
Consultant: Dr Brian Bowers, Senior Research Fellow
at the Science Museum, London.
Proofreader: Lindsay Barnes

Published in Great Britain in 2002 by Hodder Wayland, an imprint
of Hodder Children's Books.
This paperback edition published in 2005

British Library Cataloguing in Publication Data
Gogerly, Liz
Dian Fossey. – (Scientists Who Made History)
   1. Fossey, Dian, 1932–1985
   2. Women primatologists – United States – Biography –
Juvenile literature
   3. Primatologists – United States – Biography –
Juvenile literature
   I. Title II. Lee, Anna
   599.8'84'092

ISBN 0 7502 4008 3

Printed in China

Hodder Children's Books
A division of Hodder Headline Limited
338 Euston Road, London, NW1 3BH

Picture Acknowledgements: Corbis 8, 17, 28; Dian Fossey Gorilla Fund
4, 5, 13, 16t, 20, 22, 23, 25, 27, 30, 32, 33, 35, 39; Impact Photos 21,
38, 40; Oxford Scientific Films 16b; Popperfoto 6, 7, 12, 29;
Still Pictures 11, 14, 18, 19, 24, 26, 31, 37, 41; Topham Picturepoint
title page, 10, 34, 36; Yann Arthus Bertrand/Impact *cover*.

Contents

4   'The Place of Hands'

8   Lonely Years

10   The Call of Africa

20   The Camp at Karisoke

28   Fame and Fury

34   Gorillas in the Mist

38   The Killers in the Mist

42   The Legacy of Dian Fossey

44   Timeline

46   Glossary

47   Further Information

48   Index

'The Place of Hands'

THE SUN WAS shining brightly as Dian Fossey and *National Geographic Magazine* photographer Bob Campbell set off through the forest. They hadn't been following tracks for very long before they stumbled upon a group of gorillas that Fossey called Group 8. The animals were feeding and Fossey and Campbell watched as they chomped through the wild celery that they loved. Fossey experienced a warm glow. She felt privileged that these magnificent beasts were letting her into their lives. Peanuts, a cheeky young male, gave a quick display of branch slapping and chest beating, then lay down next to her to play.

LEFT: *A mountain gorilla in Rwanda, where Fossey carried out most of her research. Although she spent every day with the gorillas, it was three years before she made physical contact with one of these beautiful animals.*

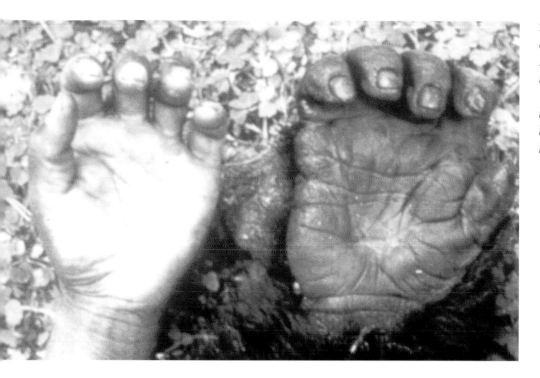

LEFT: *Fossey was overjoyed when Peanuts first touched her hand. This picture shows the similarities between a gorilla's hand and our own.*

Bob quietly photographed the pair as they began to imitate each other. Soon, Fossey lay down on the ground next to Peanuts. Gently, she extended her hand towards the waiting gorilla, letting it drop to the floor. For a moment Peanuts looked unsure. Then, driven by his overwhelming curiosity, he reached out and his hand briefly covered Fossey's palm. It had finally happened! Fossey had tears in her eyes and Peanuts was so excited that he made a proud little chest beat before bounding away into the forest. It was the first time a gorilla had dared to make contact with Fossey, and it had felt magical.

Fossey had encountered Peanuts and his group within a few months of arriving at Karisoke in Rwanda, Africa, in September 1967. Months later he'd been the first gorilla to hold Fossey's gaze. Fossey had felt a flash of recognition and acceptance – he was as intrigued by her as she was by him. Since then, she had patiently watched Peanuts grow in confidence. Her patience was rewarded when he finally touched her on that sunny day in January 1970.

IN THEIR OWN WORDS

'Often I am asked about the most rewarding experience I have ever had with gorillas. The question is extremely difficult to answer because each hour with the gorillas provides its own return and satisfaction... The [hand] contact was among the most memorable [experiences] of my life among the gorillas.'

DIAN FOSSEY DESCRIBING HER FIRST CONTACT WITH A GORILLA IN HER BOOK *GORILLAS IN THE MIST*, 1983.

WILD THEORIES

In 1859 Charles Darwin's book *The Origin of Species* shocked the world. In it, he suggested that humans may have evolved from apes. This outraged many people, who believed that God had created humans. The debate about evolution continues to rage today.

Louis Leakey

In 1959, a paleoanthropologist called Louis Leakey discovered a skull of the earliest known ancestor of man in Tanzania, Africa. Believed to be 1.75 million years old, it showed that human evolution was much older than previously thought. Leakey went on to discover the remains of the two-million year old *Homo habilis*, which he considered the true ancestor of humans (*Homo sapiens*). These skeletons enabled him to piece together how our ancient ancestors moved and looked, but Leakey wanted to find out about the evolution of human behaviour.

Leakey thought that the close study of the chimpanzee, the gorilla and the orang-utan in their natural habitat would give the key to human evolution. Studying apes to gain an insight into human behaviour wasn't a new idea, but most studies had taken place in the laboratory. Those who'd tried to study chimpanzees in the wild had failed because the animals fled as soon as people came near. However, studies of the mountain gorillas in the Belgian Congo in Africa by George Schaller in 1959–60 were promising, and in his book, *The Year of the Gorilla* (1962), Schaller wrote about his encounters with these 'amiable' (friendly) animals. Despite this success, many scientists thought Leakey was mad to consider close-up studies.

ABOVE: *Although he travelled extensively, the scientist Charles Darwin (1809–1882) had little evidence for his theories of evolution. However, most scientists now believe his ideas to be correct.*

LEFT: *Dr Louis Leakey (1903–1972) makes comparisons between the skull of a chimpanzee (left) and a skull of what is believed to be man's oldest ancestor. The human-like skull was nicknamed 'Nutcracker Man' because of its large teeth.*

His reputation didn't improve when he sent an unqualified young Englishwoman called Jane Goodall to study the chimpanzees in the wild forests of Tanzania in July 1960. Only a few years later, Fossey was to follow in her footsteps.

JANE GOODALL AND THE GORILLAS

Rather than being wild and unpredictable, Jane Goodall found that chimpanzees could be gentle with each other. They greet each other with hugs and kisses and tenderly groom each other. They also build soft, leafy nests to sleep in. She discovered that, like humans, chimpanzees sometimes hunt for meat and use natural vegetation as tools or weapons. For example, when they're eating thorny plants they use leaves to hold the stem and protect their hands. Jane recorded all her observations in journals. Rather than the accepted scientific approach, with numbers and statistics, Jane talked about the animals as individuals. Many scientists criticised this method, but none could deny its success.

IN THEIR OWN WORDS

'Dr. Leakey spoke to me most enthusiastically about Jane Goodall's excellent field work with the chimpanzees ... I believe it was at this time the seed was planted in my head ... that I would someday return to Africa to study the gorillas.'

DIAN FOSSEY WRITING ABOUT HER FIRST MEETING WITH DR. LOUIS LEAKEY IN *GORILLAS IN THE THE MIST*.

Lonely Years

DIAN FOSSEY WAS born on 16 January 1932 in Fairfax, California, near San Francisco in the United States. She was the only child of George and Kitty Fossey. When Dian was six her parents divorced, and a year later her mother married a man named Richard Price. Dian's father tried to stay in contact with her, but as his name wasn't tolerated in the Price household, they soon lost touch altogether. Dian's upbringing was very strict, and despite her pleas for a pet dog or cat, she was only ever allowed a goldfish.

Dian's lonely childhood was followed by years of working her own way through college and university. In 1950 she began a course in pre-veterinary medicine at the University

BELOW: *Fossey loved to spend time in the forests of Kentucky. It was here that she first became passionate about wildlife.*

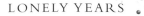

of California in Davis. Without her parents' financial backing, she had to take holiday jobs in factories, offices or laboratories. Although she was determined to work with animals she found science very difficult. When she failed her second year, she was forced to rethink her plans. By 1954 Dian had gained a degree in occupational therapy and she spent the next seven years as director of occupational therapy in a hospital for disabled children in Louisville, Kentucky.

In Kentucky, Dian found some happiness. She moved to a cottage on a farm called Glenmary on the outskirts of Louisville. Surrounded by forests and fields, Dian found she enjoyed the peace and quiet. She also discovered that watching the farm animals and wild creatures in the countryside interested her. She was slowly moving towards her true calling in life.

IN THEIR OWN WORDS

'When I wake up in the morning, I just run to the windows all over the house and am blinded by the beauty.'

DIAN FOSSEY TALKING ABOUT HER TIME AT GLENMARY FARM IN *WOMAN IN THE MISTS*, 1983.

The Call of Africa

FOR YEARS, FOSSEY had dreamed of visiting Africa. Friends returned from the African bush with exciting tales about the wild animals and she wanted to see them for herself. As usual, money was an obstacle, but she was determined to taste the wilds of Africa for herself by the end of 1963. Eventually, she decided to take out a three-year loan to fund a six-week safari to Kenya, Tanzania, Uganda and Southern Rhodesia (now Zimbabwe).

Reading about Africa and preparations for the trip occupied Fossey for the months leading up to her dream trip. One book, George Schaller's *The Year of the Gorilla*, particularly interested her. Fossey wanted to see the majestic mountain gorillas he talked about for herself, so she added the Congo (now Democratic Republic of Congo) to her itinerary. As Fossey's excitement grew, so did her fears for her health. She had always suffered from bouts of pneumonia, and was especially worried that the pneumonia that struck a month before she was due to leave would affect her plans. Despite her weakened state, Fossey boarded the plane to Kenya on 26 September 1963.

BELOW: *A photograph of a gorilla taken by George Schaller, whose work fascinated Fossey.*

ABOVE. *Africa cast its spell on Fossey. Although she fell in love with the gorillas, she was also enchanted by many other species, including the elephants and impala.*

Unsurprisingly, Fossey fell in love with Africa. Seeing animals in their natural habitats filled her with wonder. Of all the African creatures though, the mountain gorillas she saw in the Virungas Volcanoes region in the Congo moved her the most. When she heard their high-pitched screams, then finally saw them, she was overwhelmed. She knew that she'd have to return to Africa one day. A meeting with the paleoanthropologist Louis Leakey in Tanzania had added to her determination to return. Leakey had admired the gutsy American woman who claimed she wanted to return to Africa to work with the gorillas and he told her to keep in touch.

IN THEIR OWN WORDS

'I was struck by the physical magnificence of the huge jet-black bodies blended against the green ... of the thick forest foliage.'

FOSSEY REMEMBERING THE FIRST TIME SHE SAW A MOUNTAIN GORILLA IN THE WILD.

'GORILLA GIRL'

Fossey's enthusiasm for her African adventure was shown in magazine articles that were published in Louisville's *Courier Journal*, together with photographs she had taken of the mountain gorillas. However, it wasn't until three years later, in March 1966, that she had the opportunity to discuss her passion with Louis Leakey again. Leakey was visiting Louisville, and Fossey was amazed when he recognized her and requested a meeting.

Leakey had been looking for a suitable person to conduct long-term close-up research of mountain gorillas in the Virungas Volcanos. He was particularly keen on using women for his studies and felt that Jane Goodall had more than proved that women had the necessary patience and determination to do the job well. In Fossey he saw a strong-willed woman who was mature and dedicated enough to handle the rigours of living in the wilds of Africa for a long period of time. However, Fossey was shocked when Leakey concluded their meeting by suggesting that she have her appendix removed. He pointed out that appendicitis could be deadly if it struck when medical help wasn't readily available.

LEFT: *Jane Goodall makes friends with a chimpanzee in Tanzania. During her studies she made constant comparisons between human and chimp behaviour. Examples of DNA suggest the chimpanzee might be human's closest living relative.*

Fossey, who had not been offered the job officially, promptly had her appendix removed, and waited for Leakey to contact her. When his letter arrived, it was a dream come true. Leakey wanted Fossey as his 'gorilla girl' – he would find sponsors for the costs of travel and setting up a research base. In return she would write about her experiences with the gorillas. Later, he told Fossey that he'd told her to have her appendix removed only as a joke. But the determination she displayed in having the operation made him sure that he'd found the right woman for the job.

ABOVE: *Although Fossey knew that life in the the remote jungle of central Africa would be difficult, she couldn't wait to begin her work there.*

IN THEIR OWN WORDS

'There was no way that I could explain to dogs, friends, or parents my compelling need to return to Africa to launch a long-term study of gorillas. Some may call it destiny and others may call it dismaying. I call the sudden turn of events in my life fortuitous [lucky].'

DIAN FOSSEY TALKING ABOUT LEAVING THE USA
IN *GORILLAS IN THE MIST*.

INTO THE WILDERNESS

In December 1966 Fossey was on a plane bound for Africa once again. Since Leakey's letter had arrived, she'd faced more obstacles. Pneumonia struck yet again, and her parents put up strong objections to her living alone in the politically unstable Congo. But Fossey was determined. As she set off to the airport she was weighed down with four cameras, a typewriter with paper and a whole wardrobe of outdoor clothes.

Leakey had organized for Fossey to spend Christmas with Jane Goodall and her husband. Jane had been studying the chimpanzees at Gombe in Tanzania for over three years, and she gave Fossey a crash course in data collection. Then, before journeying to the Virungas, Fossey met Leakey in Kenya. There they bought a second-hand Land Rover, which Fossey later christened Lily.

MOUNTAIN GORILLAS

People have known about the existence of the gorilla since the nineteenth century, but it wasn't until 1902 that the mountain gorilla (*Gorilla gorilla beringei*) was discovered. There are two other subspecies of gorilla, called the western lowland gorilla (*Gorilla gorilla gorilla*) and the eastern lowland gorilla (*Gorilla gorilla grauen*). Mountain gorillas only live in the mountain rainforests in central Africa. They are similar to the other subspecies, but are larger and more muscular. The adult male can be 1.7 to 1.8 metres tall when standing. They live in groups that vary in size from about 3 to 38 members. A group has one adult male over 15 years old. This majestic creature is called a silverback, because of his silvery fur. He takes charge of a group that includes young adult males, several females and their offspring.

ABOVE: *A silverback mountain gorilla is usually twice as heavy as an adult female and armed with longer teeth.*

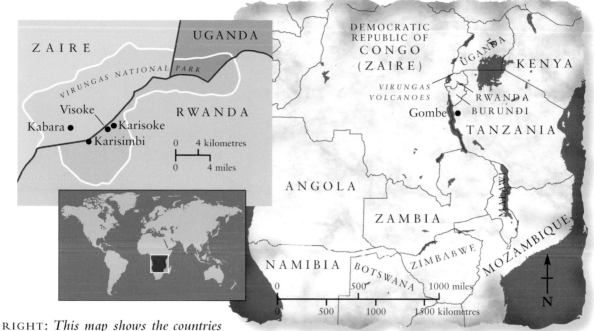

RIGHT: *This map shows the countries Fossey visited in Africa, and their neighbouring countries.*
TOP: *A map of the Virungas National Park, showing the places where Fossey lived and worked.*

Journey to the Congo

By chance, Fossey also met the photographer Alan Root while in Kenya. He accompanied her on the 700-mile trip to the Congo. They passed through dense jungle, savannah and stretches of wilderness before arriving in the heart of Africa – the Congo. Fossey was determined to go back to Kabara in the Virungas; it was where she had first seen gorillas and where George Schaller had studied the animals in 1960. It was also an area of political unrest – rebellion against the government of Congo meant that foreign travellers were in danger.

However, nothing would dampen Fossey's determination to return to Kabara. Accompanied by Alan, she hired men to take them up 4,000 feet to the Kabara meadow. At their journey's end, Fossey breathed in the sweet mountain air, looked across at the string of volcanoes and hugged herself with joy. She knew that she'd soon be with the gorillas again.

IN THEIR OWN WORDS

'There were vistas [views] along the trail that left me speechless with their majesty. The far sweep of volcanoes seemed never to end. There were some wondrous, sprawling hagenia trees lining the trail that seemed so familiar I wanted to rush up to them to shake branches.'

FOSSEY TALKS ABOUT HER RETURN TO KABARA IN *WOMAN IN THE MISTS* BY FARLEY MOWAT, 1987.

Waking up to Nature

Alan Root gave Fossey invaluable lessons in tracking, but after two days he had to leave the camp. Fossey was anxious about being alone, but her fears were eased a few days later with the arrival of Sanwekwe, a Congolese tracker. She'd met Sanwekwe on her previous trip; he'd worked for George Schaller and Fossey had admired his skills as a tracker.

ABOVE: *Fossey's camp at Kabara was far away from civilization. She had a small shortwave radio but listening to the outside world often made her feel even lonelier.*

TRACKING GORILLAS

Successful tracking of gorillas takes great patience and experience. Gorillas are terrestrial, which means that they mainly travel on the ground. They 'knuckle walk' – so they appear to walk on all fours – and they leave knuckleprints in the ground as they travel. These prints, together with trails of fresh dung and the disruption of trees and plants, provide clues to their whereabouts. Fossey discovered other ways of finding her gorillas, though. By crawling through the undergrowth close to the ground she could detect smells. The great silverbacks had a distinctive body odour, rather like strong human sweat, which clung to the vegetation.

ABOVE: *A gorilla knuckleprint.*

On the morning of 19 January 1967 Fossey and Sanwekwe left camp early and had their first lengthy gorilla sighting. For three hours they were transfixed as a group of nine gorillas went about their daily business. In between sunning themselves in the hot patches of the forest, they barked, hooted and squealed, as well as making their distinctive chest beat, which echoed through the forest making a 'pok-pok' sound. From now on, each movement and sound the animals made would be recorded and typed up by Fossey every evening. Like Jane Goodall, she didn't want to record the animals' activities as a series of ticks on a chart; she wanted to write about their everyday lives almost as if they were stories.

Life on the mountain wasn't easy. Years of frequent pneumonia had weakened Fossey's lungs and the long treks through the forests at high altitude were difficult. With her clothes constantly dampened from the misty mountain air, she also became ill more easily. She made monthly trips to the nearest village at the foot of the mountains for fresh vegetables and fruit, but these soon ran out. It was only Fossey's determination and love for the gorillas that kept her focused on her job.

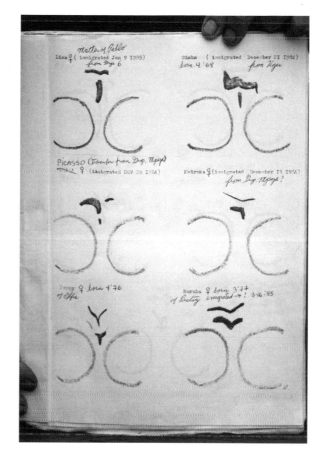

ABOVE: *A page of Fossey's handwritten notes and diagrams of gorilla noseprints. She took pleasure in recording the small details of the gorillas' behaviour and lives.*

IN THEIR OWN WORDS

'Because of the near daily encounters with elephant, buffalo, giant forest hog, and, of course, gorilla, the time spent in the field was by far more exciting than the hours, that, of necessity, had to be spent in camp. Almost immediately, I became bogged down in paperwork and have remained that way ever since.'

FOSSEY IN *GORILLAS IN THE MIST.*

FRIENDS AND FOES

It took time to gain the trust of the mountain gorillas and Fossey made mistakes. If she came too close too soon, or without warning, the silverbacks would charge at her or take their group and flee. Fossey eventually found that it was better that the gorillas saw her first and then, in their own time, they would inch closer to her. She also discovered that imitating the sounds they made was more successful than talking to them. She gradually learned which sounds gained the animals' confidence.

When Fossey began her observations, she had slapped her thighs in imitation of their chestbeats. She soon realized that this was a sign of excitement or fear for gorillas, and that it was better to copy their contentment vocalizations, which sounded like a purr. Fossey also copied the animals' movements. Scratching, pretending to eat the wild celery they liked or even crouching in a submissive position all helped to win their trust.

RIGHT: *A female gorilla beats her chest. This is usually a sign of excitement.*

GORILLA TALK

Gorillas communicate using body language and sounds. Fossey discovered 25 distinct sounds or vocalizations. She quickly learned the difference between the sounds. Roars tend to be aggressive while screams and 'wraaghs' are to raise alarm in any situation. High-pitched barking usually expresses mild alarm and curiosity – Fossey often heard this response when she was discovered hiding in the bushes. One of the most comforting sounds Fossey discovered is the belch vocalization, which often means that the gorillas are contented. She particularly enjoyed hearing the gorillas chuckle, which they do when they're playing. Sounds to communicate with other groups include the hootseries, or 'hoo-hoo-hoos', which often come before chestbeats.

As Fossey made progress with the gorillas, events in the human world began to take over. On 9 July 1967 armed Congolese soldiers arrived at the camp. A rebel leader called Moise Tshombe had taken the leadership of the eastern region of the Congo by force. The border between the Congo and Uganda had been closed and white people were being treated with great mistrust. After six months of study, Fossey was escorted down the mountain and taken into custody.

It was now too dangerous to stay in the Congo. Many people, including Leakey, pleaded with Fossey to return to the USA, but Fossey was determined to transfer her studies to a grassy clearing a short distance from Kabara in Rwanda. Rwanda is located a few miles south of the equator, and is one of the smallest countries in Africa. By 24 September 1967 Fossey had found her new research camp; it was 10,000 feet up in the Rwandan National Park, between the mountains of Karisimbi and Visoke – she called it Karisoke.

ABOVE. *A mother gorilla vocalizes to her baby. Fossey soon learned that different vocalizations had very different meanings.*

The Camp at Karisoke

THE CAMP AT Karisoke was in a clearing surrounded by forest, with a stream flowing through it. As the first tents were put up, Fossey heard gorilla chestbeats – and she knew she had found the right place for her research. However, Karisoke would be quite different from Kabara. Rwanda is a heavily populated country and its people (the Batwa, the Hutu and the Tutsi tribes) farm and graze within the national park. From now on, Fossey would make many friends within the gorilla community, but she would also make many enemies of the farmers and poachers who threatened the gorilla's natural habitat.

The most important thing to Fossey was contact with the gorillas. At Karisoke, the gorillas were more wary of humans. After a year of study, the animals were still unused to Fossey, who would wait patiently, sitting 30 to 40 feet away.

ABOVE: *At first Fossey lived in tents at Karisoke. Later she moved into this cabin. She made curtains out of African material and put tusks, animal skins and pictures on the walls.*

IDENTIFYING GORILLAS

As Fossey began to recognize the gorillas in each group, she gave them names. She quickly found ways of distinguishing between each gorilla because every gorilla has its own noseprint (see page 17). While the noses of animals in the same group are similar, each gorilla has a slightly different nose. Fossey would make sketches of each gorilla's noseprint. Other vital clues to identification included colouring. Mountain gorillas have long fur that varies in colour from blue-black to brownish-grey. Fossey also looked out for distinguishing features such as scars or birthmarks – much the same as humans do on passports. She called her favourite gorilla Digit because he had lost a finger.

Gorilla groups

During her 18 years of research at Karisoke, Fossey encountered nine groups of gorillas. Each group was numbered and every individual was given a name. Fossey concentrated her studies on three groups; groups 4, 5 and 8. The dominant silverback, usually about twice the size of the adult females, was the leader of each group. He would lead a group through the forests, his experience determining his reaction to each situation. If the situation was threatening, he might lead his group to charge the enemy. However, Fossey found that once a silverback had grown used to her presence, the younger members of his group would come to her. It was almost as if the great silverback had allowed the youngsters out to play with a friend. Eventually, it was the silverback's trust that allowed her to observe the gorillas.

IN THEIR OWN WORDS

'Once within sight of Rafiki, the elderly female moved directly to him. They looked directly into each other's face and embraced. She placed her arm over his back and he did likewise over hers.'

DIAN FOSSEY REMEMBERING AN AFFECTIONATE MOMENT BETWEEN THE SILVERBACK RAFIKI AND THE OLD MATRIARCH, COCO, IN GROUP 8.

LEFT: *After waking at about 6am most family groups spend the morning feeding. By noon they are ready for a rest, although the youngsters often like to play.*

FAMILY TIES

All gorillas were important to Fossey, but she grew especially close to certain individuals, such as Peanuts (see pages 4–5). Of all the gorillas, Fossey's favourite was Digit of Group 4. She watched him grow and develop from a five-year–old, bouncy bundle of black fluff to a young adult who was beginning to take responsibility for protecting the group.

When Fossey first encountered Group 4 in 1967 there had been fourteen members. The silverback leader was an elderly giant she called Whinny. The group contained two senior females, as well as four young adult females, aged between six and eight. Two younger silverbacks, a few infants and young adult males, including Digit, completed the group.

ABOVE: *Members of Group 4 play in the undergrowth. Although young gorillas enjoy a game, they never venture far away from their mother.*

By 1972 Fossey was spending a great deal of time with Group 4 and had gathered much information about their behaviour. Whinny had died of natural causes in 1968, and now the fifteen-year-old silverback, Uncle Bert, was the relatively young and inexperienced leader. Uncle Bert's youthfulness meant he enjoyed playing. Playtime, Fossey discovered, was extremely important to the younger gorillas. They enjoyed leaping from tree to tree and having long wrestling matches. She loved watching their antics, and they often included her in their games, allowing her to tickle or groom them.

Unfortunately, Uncle Bert's inexperience often led Group 4 into fights with other groups. Intergroup interaction, when two different groups of gorillas come together, is a necessary part of gorilla survival. However, sexually mature females are often poached from one group to ensure the survival of another. The meetings can be violent, and many animals are injured or killed defending their groups. Eventually, Uncle Bert lost three young females to another group.

LEFT: *Fossey tried to type up her notes about the day's events every night. A rescued monkey called Kima often kept her company.*

BRINGING UP BABIES

Infant gorillas are breast-fed by their mothers until they are about two years old. Fossey especially enjoyed observing the gorillas raise their offspring. In February 1969 she heard that a baby gorilla had been trapped by poachers to send to a German zoo. She was furious, and persuaded the park guard (called a conservator) to let her take the baby back to Karisoke.

Coco and Pucker

The capture of infant gorillas is a particularly horrible business. In order to snatch a baby, many members of the gorilla group are killed as they try to protect their young.

Fossey was determined to help the rescued infant recover from its ordeal. She named it Coco and put her in a room next to her own at Karisoke. The room was decorated with forest vegetation that gorillas particularly like to eat, and soft vegetation on which Coco could nest. Once they were alone, Fossey opened Coco's pen. To her amazement, Coco crawled onto her lap. Later, when Coco looked out the window at the mountains, she started sobbing. It would be the only time that Fossey saw a gorilla cry.

LEFT: *A baby gorilla eating leaves. Fossey fed Coco and Pucker a natural diet of wild celery, thistles and nettles.*

Fossey dedicated herself to Coco's survival. She reassured the frightened animal with gorilla vocalizations, and sometimes cuddled her to sleep. Like a human child, Coco responded to the warmth and feeling of security. A week later she was making a steady recovery when another baby gorilla was brought to the camp. Pucker had been captured as a replacement for the German zoo. All eight of her family group had died trying to save her.

Months of loving attention saved both gorillas, but Fossey knew she couldn't prevent them from being sent to Germany. When the time came for their departure, Fossey packed the last forest vegetation she knew they would ever eat into their cage. Through the years Fossey saw photographs and heard stories about her 'wild orphans'. They looked and sounded depressed. Then in 1978, aged just ten, Coco and Pucker died within a month of each other.

BELOW: *Fossey stroking a gorilla's foot. After her experience with Coco and Pucker, she often used touch to communicate with the gorillas.*

IN THEIR OWN WORDS

'After a few weeks I changed approaches from mild "tickle-tickles" to drawn-out "ouchy-gouchy-goo-zoooom" ... The term "ouchy-gouchy-goo-zoooom" is not in any dictionary, yet it seems to be an international ... term that can evoke laughter and smiles from both human and nonhuman primates.'

DIAN FOSSEY WRITING ABOUT THE TICKLING GAMES SHE ENJOYED WITH COCO AND PUCKER IN *GORILLAS IN THE MIST*.

THE FIGHT FOR LIFE

When Fossey founded Karisoke she knew that the local people herded cattle and hunted within the park. She told them that she would not tolerate either activity in the study areas. Friends tried to make her see sense; the locals, after all, had always herded cattle in the park and they hunted for meat to feed their families. Fossey argued that they kept too many cattle and began herding away the cattle that strayed onto 'her' area. She also destroyed any traps she found laid down by the poachers. They not only killed the wildlife, she reasoned, they also trapped the gorillas.

Fossey grew angrier when it became clear that gorillas were becoming game for the tourist trade. Not only did poachers catch infants to sell overseas to zoos, but they killed adult gorillas to sell as body parts – ashtrays made from gorilla's hands were particularly popular. In 1970, while Fossey was away in England, she heard about the massacre of five adult gorillas on the outskirts of the park. There was little Fossey could do but write angry letters to the park director and conservation organizations.

RIGHT: *A poacher sets an animal trap. Gorillas were often caught in wire-traps or deep pit traps with pointed stakes at the bottom.*

LEFT: *This gorilla has lost a hand in a snare. Some gorillas die later from an infection from their injuries.*

The local people were already suspicious of Fossey. They called her Nyiramachabelli – the old woman who lives alone in the forest without a man. Now she became even more unpopular as she took the herding and poaching problem into her own hands. In July 1973, after driving cattle into a local settlement, she pulled a gun on locals. On other occasions she shot at and killed cattle. Sometimes she held poachers hostage and bullied them into revealing information about their employers. She'd then spook them using halloween masks and fire-crackers as she pretended to be a witch. The locals believed in black magic, or *sumu* as they called it, and began to fear and dislike this unpredictable woman.

Fame and Fury

IN ORDER TO receive further grants for her research, Fossey needed a Ph.D. (Doctorate in Philosophy). Between January 1970 and 1976, when her thesis was accepted, she made regular trips to Cambridge University in England to gain a doctorate in zoology. Her dissertation was based upon her research into the gorillas. She had to be away from Africa for months at a time and missed the gorillas terribly. As the poachers moved in and her conservation work became more important, she was forced to recruit researchers to continue her work during her absence. However, not everybody had the same commitment to conservation as Fossey, and this added to her worries while she was away.

The National Geographic Society had always supported Fossey's work by paying for the upkeep of the camp. In return, her story and the progress of her research was regularly featured in the *National Geographic Magazine*.

LEFT: *Fossey spent her time at Cambridge University studying and worrying about the gorillas back at Karisoke.*

ABOVE:
This photograph of Fossey and the gorillas was taken for the National Geographic Society. Such pictures helped develop public interest in Fossey's work.

In the January 1970 issue, beautiful colour photographs of the gorillas in their natural habitat had introduced Fossey and her work to the world. She was filmed by the National Geographic Society in 1968, 1969 and 1970, and in later years television cameras from around the world filmed the gorillas. In 1978 the British television presenter David Attenborough was filmed with the gorillas for the BBC *Life on Earth* series. Now everybody could see for themselves what Fossey already knew – that these majestic creatures were as gentle as they were strong, and that there was a recognition between our two species that went both ways.

Fossey hated the disturbance to the lives of the gorillas that such publicity brought, but she recognized there could be a benefit. When poaching became a serious problem, she threatened to use her fame to generate international disapproval. It was a promise she kept. She also insisted she'd find out who was behind the killings. Dian Fossey was not only becoming famous, she was turning into a serious threat to the Rwandan authorities. From now on, they started to monitor her movements.

IN THEIR OWN WORDS

'In their greed to obtain photographs, tourists and uninvited film crews came to pose almost as much of a threat to the gorillas as poachers did. One French film team ... relentlessly pursued Group 5 daily for six weeks. The trauma caused Effie to abort [lose her unborn baby].'

FOSSEY IN *GORILLAS IN THE MIST*, 1983.

DEATH OF A GENTLE FRIEND

'If I was alone, he often invited play by flopping over onto his back, waving stumpy legs in the air, and looking at me smilingly as if to say, "How can you resist me?" At such times, I fear, my scientific detachment dissolved.'

DIAN FOSSEY WRITING ABOUT DIGIT IN *GORILLAS IN THE MIST*.

In January 1978 Fossey had been preparing to receive David Attenborough and the BBC film crew. She wanted to make a good impression, but by the time the BBC had arrived there had been a terrible discovery. On 31 December 1977, the poachers targeted one of Fossey's gorilla groups – Group 4 – for the first time. Digit was now ten years old, and was taking some responsibility for defending the group. It seemed that he had been attacked as he fought off the poachers. When his body was discovered in early January 1978, it had been hacked almost beyond recognition. Fossey was wracked with grief. She replayed the scenes of their friendship in her mind. She remembered him as the gentle and curious animal who'd lain his head in her lap. She was now more determined than ever to put a stop to the poachers.

RIGHT: *Fossey's favourite gorilla Digit had been filmed by the* National Geographic *as he rolled over and slept. It is possible that his trust in human beings made him an easy target for the poachers.*

Fossey wrote to the Rwandan President, Major General Juvenal Habyarimana, telling him that she would contact every conservation society she could reach in her quest to protect the gorillas. She would ask them to pressure the Rwandan government to cut funds to the park conservator and guards, as they didn't do their job. She also suggested that stronger penalties such as long prison sentences or even death for the poachers might deter their actions.

Later, Fossey mounted a poster campaign that showed Digit's mutilated body, saying 'Come and Visit Me in Rwanda'. It was a copy of a poster that had used a photograph of Digit to promote tourism in Rwanda. Finally, she launched an international fund-raising campaign that would become known as the Digit Fund. The money collected would be used for anti-poaching patrols. From now on Fossey's work would centre on active conservation. This would prove to be a dangerous business that would make her many enemies.

ABOVE: *Fossey's anti-poaching campaign helped to raise awareness of the dangers of poaching throughout Africa. This anti-poaching patrol is working in Tanzania, which shares a border with Rwanda.*

MAKING ENEMIES

Sadly, the anti-poaching patrols could not be put in place quickly enough to save other members in Group 4. Uncle Bert, the silverback leader, and a young mother called Macho were shot in July 1978. The poachers wanted to snatch Macho's son, Kweli, but miraculously Fossey later found the infant. However, without its silverback leader, Group 4 was in danger of poaching from other groups. In time, the group would cease to exist.

'She was very wary about entering into a relationship. The gorillas ... were honest in their feelings towards her. If they were angry, you could see they were angry; if they liked you, they showed it. It was very up front. Fossey appreciated the honesty of the relationship you have with gorillas, and you don't owe them anything and they don't owe you anything, other than trust. With the gorillas she didn't have to hide her feelings from them.'

IAN REDMOND, FOSSEY'S FRIEND AND COLLEAGUE, FROM *WALKING WITH THE GREAT APES* BY SY MONTGOMERY.

RIGHT: *Fossey organizes an anti-poaching patrol at Karisoke. She declared all-out war against the poachers, whom she believed were responsible for the deaths of two-thirds of the gorillas in her study area.*

Fossey's fragile health began to suffer again. Over the years, climbing at such high altitudes made her out of breath, and she'd been struck by many illnesses including rabies, dysentery and pneumonia. Furthermore, the loss of so many gorillas to poachers made her angry and depressed.

Some people felt Fossey's behaviour was becoming increasingly unpredictable and irresponsible. She was suspicious of everybody, including the park conservator. She thought he might be employing poachers, then using the slaughter of animals as a reason to ask for more funding for the park. She also discriminated against African project workers who were helping with her research. If the gorillas became used to black researchers, she believed they would be less likely to run from poachers, who were also black. This reasoning seemed racist and angered the people in whose land she was actually a visitor.

Fossey was also increasingly against the gorilla safaris that had become an important part of Rwandan tourism. She was particularly upset that Group 5 had moved from the safety of the poacher-free zone to the outskirts of the park to avoid the tourists. By 1979, many people thought it would be better for the future of Karisoke if Fossey left. With Fossey in charge, funding was becoming a problem. Because of the bad publicity, even the National Geographic Society was keen for Fossey to leave Rwanda.

ABOVE: *Gorillas often have mannerisms or facial expressions that are similar to humans', which makes them especially appealing to tourists. Fossey believed that tourism posed a major threat to the gorillas' survival.*

Gorillas in the Mist

WITHOUT HELP FROM the National Geographic
Society, Fossey realized she would have to leave Karisoke. An
offer to teach at Cornell University in Ithaca, New York in
1980 gave her a reason to leave. While in the United States
she could also write her book, which she later called *Gorillas
in the Mist*. Fossey's portrait of her life and the lives of the
gorillas she watched for thirteen years is an absorbing
adventure story. It introduces the different family groups and
the 'wild orphans' Coco and Pucker. When *Gorillas in the
Mist* was published in 1983 the book was an international
success. Fossey was delighted that she had been able to bring
the gorillas to life for so many readers.

ABOVE: *Cornell University, where Fossey taught for several years in
the early 1980s.*

LEFT: *Sandy Harcourt (left) with another researcher and Fossey (right). Harcourt ran Karisoke while Fossey was in the USA.*

During these years in the USA, Fossey managed to re-build her strength. Despite her severely damaged lungs and bad back, the call of Africa was still strong. She worried about the state of Karisoke, which was being run in her absence by a scientist called Sandy Harcourt. Fossey distrusted his more scientific approach to research, and she particularly worried about the plight of the gorillas.

News that another silverback had been slaughtered trying to protect its young reached her in December 1982. Fossey was desperate to fly out immediately, but because of her work at Cornell, she wouldn't return to Karisoke until the following June. On her arrival in Karisoke, Fossey found that the gorillas needed her more than ever. The camp had been badly neglected by the visiting scientists and Fossey despaired at the work ahead of her. Her spirits were lifted by a warm welcome from Group 5. When the whole group came to meet her she was ecstatic – she was finally home!

IN THEIR OWN WORDS

'She stared intently into my eyes, and it was eye-to-eye contact for thirty or forty seconds. Not knowing quite what to do, for I had never had this reaction from gorillas before, I squished myself flat on the bed of vegetation. Whereupon she smelled my head and neck, then lay down beside me ... and embraced me! ... GOD, she did remember.'

FOSSEY'S THRILLED RESPONSE TO MEETING HER OLD FRIEND, TUCK.

THE FIGHT GOES ON

Towards the end of August 1983, Fossey was attending lecture tours in the United States to publicize *Gorillas in the Mist*. While there, she came up with a new way to protect the gorillas. She called it the Guardians for Gorillas Groups plan. People from overseas would adopt a gorilla group, and the money raised would be used to pay local people to protect the gorillas. By paying them to protect the animals, the locals would have no need to poach them anymore.

LEFT: *The strain of another promotional tour for* Gorillas in the Mist *shows on Fossey's face in this photograph from February 1984. By the end of the month she was back at Karisoke again.*

Meanwhile, the research project at Karisoke went bankrupt and was in danger of being closed down. By December, Fossey was back in Karisoke and in control. Using the money she'd earned on the lecture tour and proceeds from her book, she managed to pay the camp staff and trackers who kept the camp going. Money from the Digit Fund meant that anti-poaching patrols still managed to ruin traps and protect the gorillas from poachers, too.

With Fossey's health becoming worse, it grew more difficult for her to visit the gorillas in the mountains. She was particularly worried about their changing behaviour and the shifting social structure within the groups. It was usual for young males to split off to form new groups, but now female members of groups were leaving groups to search for males. This unusual behaviour was creating friction within the groups. Fossey called these strange episodes 'Gorilla Soap Opera', but she was deeply concerned about the long-term effects upon the gorilla community due to humans taking over their habitat.

ABOVE: *A gorilla mother and baby. Dian missed the gorillas terribly while she was in the United States.*

IN THEIR OWN WORDS

'I'm going to die and the gorillas will all die around me. They'll be gone within ten years.'

FOSSEY'S PREDICTION FOR HERSELF AND THE GORILLAS, FROM *WALKING WITH THE GREAT APES* BY SY MONTGOMERY.

The Killers in the Mist

IN MAY 1985 the anti-poaching patrols caught a well-known poacher called Sebahutu. Fossey tied him up in her living room for a day until he gave her the names of sixty poachers, as well as others who were involved in the selling of animals. There were many important people on that list. Perhaps it was Sebahutu's information that would eventually endanger Fossey's life.

ABOVE: *The last pictures of Fossey were taken outside her hut in Karisoke with camp workers and anti-poaching patrollers. In front of them is a giant pile of snares and traps they have collected.*

However, Fossey was preoccupied with raising money for Karisoke, and in June she left for the USA to collect money raised by the Digit Fund. While she was away the Rwandan president's son had visited Karisoke. He had been told that Fossey was keeping tourists away from the gorillas. As the gorilla safaris were an important part of Rwanda's income, he was angry.

On Fossey's return to Karisoke, a series of weird events had an unsettling effect on her. She had always taken the local's use of black magic seriously. Years earlier when she had discovered that her hair was being collected for use in spells against her she began to clean her hairbrush every night. In October 1985, when her pet parrots were poisoned, she began to feel afraid. Later, when she found a wooden carving of a puff adder, a venomous species of snake, she knew that the locals were practising their black magic upon her – a puff adder was a death curse!

Fossey's health was becoming even worse; she was now coughing up blood. Her health had been so bad for years that there was no reason to suspect witchcraft was the cause, but Fossey still wondered … However, even Fossey could not have guessed what would follow. After spending a quiet Christmas at Karisoke, Fossey was brutally murdered in her hut on 27 December 1985.

IN THEIR OWN WORDS

'When you realize the value of all life, you dwell less on what is past and concentrate more on the preservation of the future.'

FOSSEY'S FINAL LETTER TO HER FRIEND
ROSAMUND CARR, 22 DECEMBER 1985.

ABOVE: *Fossey's living room had been her sanctuary. The walls were covered in photographs of her friends, the gorillas. Her body was found in the next room, beside her bed.*

THE END IN SIGHT

Fossey was buried next to Digit on 31 December 1985, in the little gorilla graveyard that she had started. Her simple gravestone was engraved with the words 'No one loved gorillas more'.

The mystery of who killed Dian Fossey still rages today. In August 1986 an ex-employee of Karisoke called Emmanuel Rwelekana, and Wayne McGuire, an American researcher, were charged with the murder. By this time McGuire had fled to the USA and within weeks Rwelekana was found hanged in his cell. Many people believe both men were scapegoats, and suggest that poachers killed Fossey. Names in high places were probably passed to Fossey by the poacher Sebahutu, and some believe she was silenced before she could reveal them. There is also the theory that Fossey had to be stopped before she threatened gorilla tourism. Unfortunately the truth will probably never be known.

ABOVE: *Fossey always said she would like to be buried in the gorilla graveyard. Today the plot is almost overgrown with trees and shrubs.*

Fossey's love for the gorillas is a lasting legacy. The Digit Fund is now known as the Dian Fossey Gorilla Fund. Through sponsorship of the gorillas and fund-raising activities, it supports scientific research projects and field studies. This data advances our knowledge of the gorillas and helps conservationists understand how best to do their work.

Anti-poaching activities are still vital, but now local people are actively involved in protecting the gorilla. Through small-scale businesses based around the gorilla habitat, they have found a means of making a living – their survival is based upon the gorillas' survival.

The task is made difficult by the civil war which has been raging on and off in Rwanda since 1994. Since this time workers at Karisoke have had to leave on countless occasions. With an estimated 650 mountain gorillas left in central Africa, war has now become as serious a threat to the gorillas' survival as poaching, destruction of their natural habitat and human activities.

ABOVE: *A tourist quietly watches the antics of two young gorillas. It isn't always possible to visit the gorillas now but we can help to conserve them by supporting the Dian Fossey Gorilla Fund.*

IN THEIR OWN WORDS

'If we do not act now to protect them, most populations of great ape will become extinct within the next twenty years.'

A VIEW PUT FORWARD BY THE SPEAKERS AT THE LAUNCH OF *2001-AN APE ODYSSEY* FROM *DIGIT NEWS*, THE MAGAZINE FOR THE DIAN FOSSEY GORILLA FUND, WINTER 2000.

The Legacy of Dian Fossey

IN THEIR OWN WORDS

'This goes beyond the bounds of strict science ... Just after Fossey's death, three gorilla groups who had been at some distance from Visoke suddenly homed in on the mountain. One group travelled almost continually for two days to arrive in the vicinity.'

THE SCIENTIST IAN REDMOND TOLD THIS STORY AT THE NATIONAL GEOGRAPHIC MEMORIAL BENEFIT TO FOSSEY. HE'D BEEN ASKED HOW THE GORILLAS HAD REACTED TO FOSSEY'S DEATH (FROM *WALKING WITH THE GREAT APES* BY SY MONTGOMERY).

DIAN FOSSEY WAS the first scientist to conduct a long-term close-up study of the mountain gorillas in their natural habitat in central Africa. Her pioneering work in the field means we now know something of their family structure, their behaviour, including body language and vocalizations, their diet and their favoured habitat. In her book *Gorillas in the Mist* she introduced us to these gentle creatures that share 98 per cent of our genes and so many of our own characteristics.

The Human Ape

While Fossey was working in the field, other scientists were publishing work about human behaviour. In 1967 the British scientist Desmond Morris wrote a best-selling book *The Human Ape*. This enjoyable book traced human behaviour back to our animal ancestors. Ultimately our fascination with ourselves has become another reason to

RIGHT: *The mountain gorilla is an endangered species. The future of young gorillas such as this one depends on ongoing conservation efforts.*

PRIMATE EYES

By making comparisons with other primates, humans continue to gain an insight into our evolution. In 2001 scientists in Japan were trying to understand why humans have white around the iris of the eye, while in other primates the same area is dark. In the past, scientists believed that apes had dark eyes to protect them from the sun. They've since discovered that nocturnal primates also have dark eyes and have concluded that the darkness of the eye is to disguise the animal's direction of gaze – in other words it's a defence mechanism. With humans the eyes have great social significance. Looking into the eyes of the person you're talking to gives further information about what they are thinking.

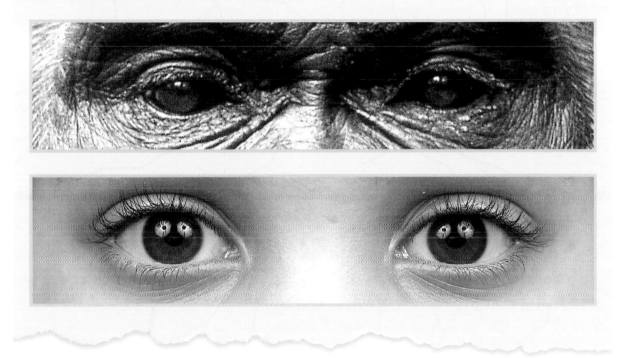

understand and protect our fellow primates. Each year we try to understand more about our evolution by discovering more about apes. Scientists have tried to find out if apes could speak. They have discovered that these highly intelligent creatures do not have the right organs to talk, but that they can learn sign language. We are still trying to discover who our closest relatives are – the gorilla or the chimpanzee. With only 650 mountain gorillas left in the world, we are running out of time. But the most important thing is saving the gorillas from extinction for their own sake.

Timeline

470 BC

What was probably the first written reference to gorillas is found in an autographical book called *The Voyage of Hanno the Carthaginian*.

1625

An English explorer called Andrew Battell writes about an encounter with a strange animal, possibly a gorilla, in West Africa.

1758

Carl Linnaeus recognizes the close relationship between humans, monkeys and apes. He classified these species as primates.

1847

American missionary, Thomas Savage and anatomist Jeffries Wyman discover a new species of ape, called a gorilla.

Circa 1857

American traveller Paul Belloni du Chaillu attempts what is probably the first ever gorilla hunt using guns. He wrote: 'He reminded me of nothing but some hellish dream creature – a being of that hideous order, half-man, half-beast.'

1859

Charles Darwin publishes *On the Origin of Species by Means of Natural Selection or the Preservation of Favoured Races in the Struggle for Life*.

1871

Charles Darwin publishes *The Descent of Man*.

1902

A German army officer called Captain Oscar von Beringe shoots two unknown species of ape while climbing Mount Sabinyo in the Virungas Volcanoes. One body was recovered and it became the type specimen – the specimen against which other specimens would be compared in future scientific research – for *Gorilla gorilla beringei* – or mountain gorilla.

1931

Louis Leakey begins archaeological digs at Olduvi Gorge in Tanzania. Ancient tools are discovered.

1932

16 JANUARY: Dian Fossey is born in Fairfax, California, USA.

1938

Fossey's parents, George and Kitty are divorced.

1950

Fossey studies as a pre-veterinary medical student at the University of California.

1954

Fossey graduates from San Jose State College with a degree in occupational therapy.

1959

Louis Leakey's wife, Mary Leakey, discovers bones of a species of early man called *Zinjanthropus*.

1959–60

George Schaller first observes mountain gorillas at Kabara.

1960

Louis Leakey discovers the skull, hands and feet of a species called *Homo habilis*.
Jane Goodall arrives at Gombe in Tanzania to begin field studies of chimpanzees.

1963

SEPTEMBER: Fossey first visits Africa where she meets Dr Louis Leakey and visits the gorillas at Kabara in the Congo.

1966

MARCH: Fossey meets Dr Louis Leakey at a lecture in Louisville.
DECEMBER: Fossey returns to Kabara, within the Parc des Virungas (Virungas Park) in the Democratic Republic of the Congo in Africa to begin studying the mountain gorillas.

1967

JULY: Fossey is forced to leave Kabara.
SEPTEMBER: Fossey founds the Karisoke Research Centre.

1968

JANUARY: Fossey writes to Louis Leakey to tell him she has chalked up 485 hours of observation of the mountain gorillas.

JUNE/JULY: Alan Root from the *National Geographic* films Fossey and the gorillas. He is replaced by Bob Campbell in August.

AUGUST: Fossey's father, George, commits suicide.

1969

FEBRUARY: Fossey saves the lives of Coco and Pucker, the two orphaned gorillas stolen by poachers for a German zoo.

1970

JANUARY: Fossey makes first human contact with a mountain gorilla called Peanuts. Fossey starts studying for a Ph.D. at Cambridge University, England.

1972

Louis Leakey dies.

1977

DECEMBER: Digit is murdered. Fossey subsequently starts the Digit Fund to raise money for anti-poaching activities.

1978

JANUARY: David Attenborough and the BBC film crew encounter the mountain gorillas.

JULY: The bodies of Uncle Bert and Macho from Group 4 are found. They'd been murdered by poachers.

1979

FEBRUARY: Fossey receives a cable from the *National Geographic*. It expresses concern at her anti-poaching activities. A few days later the US Secretary of State cabled the ambassador to Rwanda to request that Fossey leave Rwanda.

1980

Fossey begins teaching at Cornell University in Ithaca, New York.

1981

APRIL: Dian Fossey, Jane Goodall and Birute Galdikas (Louis Leakey's 'trimates') present a lecture at Sweet Briar College in Virginia, USA. The subject is 'What We Can Learn About Humankind From the Apes'.

1983

JUNE: Fossey returns to Karisoke for the first time in three years.

AUGUST: *Gorillas in the Mist* is published.

1984

OCTOBER: Fossey is presented with the Joseph Wood Krutch Medal in recognition of her work with the gorillas at the Human Society's convention in San Diego, USA.

1985

Fossey appears on the US television show 'Tonight' with Johnny Carson.

27 DECEMBER: Fossey is murdered.

31 DECEMBER: Fossey is buried in the gorilla graveyard in Karisoke.

1986

American Ruth Morris Keesling sets up Morris Animal Foundation's Mountain Gorilla Veterinary Centre in Rwanda.

1988

The film *Gorillas in the Mist* tells the story of Fossey's life. It is an international success.

1990

Karisoke is evacuated as civil war in Rwanda begins.

1994

Karisoke is evacuated once more as the civil war in Rwanda escalates.

1996

The Dian Fossey Gorilla Fund launches a new project at Mount Tshiaberimu in Congo and a community conservation programme in Rwanda.

Glossary

Appendicitis An infection of the appendix that is very painful and requires surgery to remove the appendix.

Assassination The planned murder of a person – usually somebody famous.

Black magic Magic used for evil purposes.

Bush, the Land that is covered in native trees and shrubs or other vegetation, and that usually has a low human population.

Civil war War between rival groups within one nation, usually because of religious or political differences.

Conservator Somebody who protects nature and wildlife.

Data collection The collection of information, such as measurements and different behaviour, for scientific purposes.

Defence mechanism Behaviour, such as barking when frightened, or characteristics like giving off unpleasant smells when attacked, that help animals protect themselves during confrontations with other animals.

Doctorate The highest university degree in any subject.

DNA The chemicals inside plant and animal cells in which the genes are found.

Dysentry A disease of the intestines that causes diarrhoea with blood.

Evolution The process by which a species (both animals and plants) develops from earlier forms.

Extinction When an entire species of animal or plant has died out completely.

Foliage Leaves.

Game Animals that are hunted for their meat.

Genes The things inside animal and plant cells that determine what they will be like, for example, in humans there are genes for eye, skin and hair colour.

Gorilla safaris Specially organized trips for tourists to see the mountain gorillas in their natural habitat.

Homo sapiens The scientific term used to describe the most modern representation of human beings.

Homo habilis The scientific term used to describe an early representation of human beings.

High altitude Usually refers to land that is above 3660 metres. Being at high altitude can cause sickness, headaches and shortness of breath.

Itinerary A plan for travel, including routes and times of journeys to be made.

Knuckleprints The impression left by the knuckles of an animal on a surface, for example in the soil.

Massacre The savage killing of large numbers of people or animals.

Matriarch A female of a species who is the head of the group.

Natural habitat The place where animals can live freely with access to their normal diet and surroundings.

Nocturnal Animals that are active at night.

Occupational therapy The professional treatment of people with physical, social or emotional problems.

Paleoanthropologist Someone who studies the origins, physical characteristics, behaviour and social relationships of primates.

Pneumonia A serious lung disease.

Poacher Somebody who illegally hunts animals or fish.

Political unrest When the politics of a country make its citizens likely to revolt.

Pre-veterinary medicine Medicines used to treat farm and domestic animals.

Primates A group of mammals that includes lemurs, tarsiers, monkeys, apes and humans.

Savannah Grassland area with a few trees and shrubs.

Scapegoat A person who is made to take the blame for somebody else's wrongdoings.

Sponsors A group or company that provides money to support a cause or charity.

Statistics Information and facts expressed as numbers or percentages.

Submissive Obedient and willing to give in to others.

Subspecies A term used to classify animals. Gorilla, for example, is the name of the species. The subspecies of gorilla are western lowland, eastern lowland and mountain.

Swahili A language of East Africa that is the official language of Kenya and Tanzania but used widely in central Africa too.

Thesis An extended essay based on research that is submitted as part of a degree or diploma.

Tracker A person who is specially trained to search for wild animals by following scents or marks such as footprints.

Vegetation A collective word for plants.

Vocalizations Expressions of different moods by using voices or noises.

Zoology The study of animals.

Further Information

BOOKS FOR YOUNGER READERS

Groundbreakers: Scientists and Inventors: Dian Fossey by Richard and Sara Wood (Heinemann, 2003)

BOOKS FOR OLDER READERS

Gorillas in the Mist by Dian Fossey (Phoenix, 2001)

Eyewitness Guide to Gorilla, Monkey and Ape by Ian Redmond (Dorling Kindersley, 2000)

Walking with the Great Apes by Sy Montgomery (Houghton Mifflin, 1992)

Woman in the Mists by Farley Mowat (Abacus, 1994)

WEBSITES

http://animals.about.com/library/ weekly/
An interesting site that gives background information about the mountain gorillas.

The website addresses (URLs) included in this book were valid at the time of going to press. However, because of the nature of the Internet, it is possible that some addresses may have changed, or sites may have changed or closed down since publication. While the authors and Publishers regret any inconvenience this may cause the readers, no responsibility for any such changes can be accepted by either the author or the Publisher.

ORGANIZATIONS

The Dian Fossey Gorilla Fund
110 Gloucester Avenue
London NW1 8HX
Tel: 020 7483 2681
Website: http://www.DianFossey.org

You can adopt a gorilla or give to this charity for the mountain gorillas. A newsletter called *Digit News* is published a couple of times a year. It gives an update on the current situation for the gorillas in Rwanda, including exciting snippets such as the birth of new gorillas.

Index

Page numbers in **bold** are pages where there is a photograph or an illustration.

A

Africa (see also Congo, Rwanda) 5, 6, 7, 10, 11, 12, 13, 14, 15, 28, 42
anti-poaching 31, **31**, 32, **32**, 37, 38, **38**, 41
Attenborough, David 29, 30, 45

B

black magic 27, 39

C

Cambridge University 28, **28**, 44
Campbell, Bob 4, 45
chimpanzees 7, 8, 14
Coco 21, 24, 25, 34, 44
Congo, the 7, 11, **13**, 15, 19
conservation 26, 28, 31, **33**, 43
Cornell University 34, **34**, 44

D

Darwin, Charles 6, **6**, 44
Dian Fossey Gorilla Fund 41, 45
Digit Fund 31, 38, 45

E

evolution 6, 7, 43
  human ancestry **5**, 6, **7**, 42

F

Fossey, Dian
  birth 8, 44
  childhood 8
  death 39, 45
  education 8
  health 10, 14, 17, 33, 35, 37, 39
  legacy of 41, 42
  occupational therapist, as 9
  university teaching 34, **34**, 35, 45

G

Goodall, Jane 6, 7, **12**, 14, 17, 44
Gorillas in the Mist 34, 36, **36**, 42, 45

K

Kabara 13, 15, **16**, 18, 19, 20, 44
Kenya 10, 14, 15, **15**

L

Leakey, Dr Louis 6, 7, **7**, 11, 12, 14, 19, 44, 45

M

mountain gorillas
  chestbeating 4, 5, 17, 18, **18**, 19, 20
  discovery of 14
  eyes 43, **43**
  feeding 4, 18, **21**, 24, **24**
  fights 23
  grooming 6, 23
  identification of 20
  infants 24, **24**, 25, 26, **42**
  playing 4, 21, **22**, 23, 25, 30
  social/family structure of 21, 37, 42
  species of 14
  tracking of 16, **16**
  vocalizations 18, 19, **19**, 21, 25, 42
Morris, Desmond 42

N

National Geographic Magazine 4, 28
National Geographic Society 29, **29**, 33, 34, 45

P

Peanuts 4, **4**, 5, **5**, 22, 45
poaching 20, 23, 24, 26, **26**, 27-33, 36, 37, 38, 40, 41, 45
protection 36, 37, 41
Pucker 24, 25, 34, 44

R

research 13, 17, 21, **23**
Rwanda 5, 20
  civil war in 41, 45
  gorilla tourism in 31, 33, 38, 40, **41**
  Karisoke 5, 19, 20, **20**, 24, 26, 28, 33, 35, **35**, 37, **38**, 39, 41, 45

S

Sanwekwe 16, 17
Schaller, George 7, 10, 15, 16, 44

T

Tanzania 6, 7, 11, 12, **12**, 14, **15**, **31**, 44

U

University of California 8

V

Virungas Mountain Range 11, 12, **13**, 14, 15, **15**, 44